Copyright © 2015 Candy Phelps

Available from Amazon.com, CreateSpace.com, and other retail outlets.

Book design & illustration by Candy Phelps

www.icandy-graphics.com

www.growyourseo.net

Edited by Josh Klemons

www.reverbalcommunications.com

#GROWYOURSEO

#SEOGARDEN

Dedication:

This book is dedicated to Tim: the man who taught me everything I know about gardening, the man who just brought me a homemade chocolate chip cookie while I am working late on this book, and the man who makes every day the best day ever.

I would also like to thank my parents, Bob and Kitty, and my sisters, April and Tara. I am very blessed to have so much love, support and guidance.

Thanks for showing me anything is possible with a positive attitude and a little work!

Table of Contents

Chapter 1: Introduction...7

Chapter 2: Anatomy of a Search Engine Results Page.....13

Chapter 3: Why Is SEO So Important?............................18

Chapter 4: Grandmas, Gardening & SEO.....................23

Chapter 5: Quantity + Quality Is Critical........................26

Chapter 6: Relevance is Imperative..............................35

Chapter 7: Organization Is Important............................42

Chapter 8: Good Design Gets You Far..........................46

Chapter 9: Easy Access Is Crucial.................................55

Chapter 10: Longevity Is an Advantage.......................62

Chapter 11: Reputation Is Everything............................69

Conclusion..76

CHAPTER 1

INTRODUCTION

Search Engines & SEO

T he world wide web holds over a trillion pages, according to Wired magazine founder Kevin Kelly[1]. About 570 new websites are created every minute, says one PC Magazine study[2]. These numbers are as difficult to comprehend as they are to quantify. There is a mind boggling amount of information on the Internet, and more is being created every second. So the question on everyone's mind is, "How can I get more traffic to my website?"

The answer is: Search Engine Optimization (SEO).

Before digging into SEO, we must first establish a basic understanding of what search engines are and why they exist. Search engines are computer robots "or spiders" constantly scanning and indexing the Internet. Search engines exist to help users (i.e. real human beings) find relevant content they are searching for on the web. With the nearly infinite amount of information on the Internet, we must have a way to sort and make sense of it. Search engines act much like interactive library card catalogs in helping us to do so. They help users find what they are looking for.

Google, the world's most powerful search engine, processes on average over 40,000 search queries every second[3]. How did I find this out? Of course, I "Googled" it! Google is to search engines as Kleenex is to tissue paper. They are often used synonymously, and while not technically accurate, I will occasionally do so throughout this book. I will also use the word "Google" as a verb, meaning to search using a search engine.

When you "Google" a word (aka a keyword or keyword phrase), the search engine returns a list of websites on a Search Engine Results Page (SERP) with short descriptions and links for the user to choose from.

Now that we have a basic understanding of how search engines are used, let's take a closer look at Search Engine Optimization. SEO is the process of making improvements on and off a particular website with the goal of gaining more exposure on SERPs returned by a specific query. The ultimate goal of SEO is to gain first-page, top-place ranking in the "organic" search results for a specific keyword (or group of keywords). The organic search results are free, earned positions, and the No. 1 ranking on the first page of a Google SERP gets the lion's share of the traffic. More exposure in SERPs ultimately leads to more visitors finding your website. More visitors finding your site means more customers and revenue for your business.

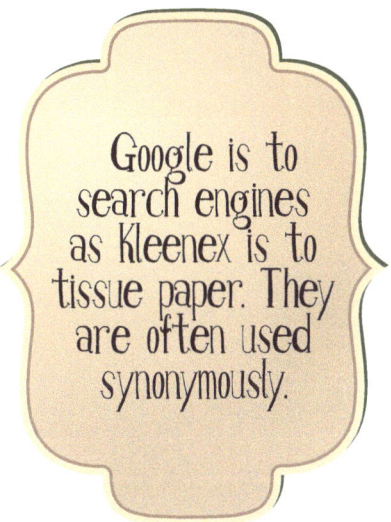

Google is to search engines as Kleenex is to tissue paper. They are often used synonymously.

The SEO industry is ever evolving, and the process of SEO is governed by extremely complex, "algorithms" (page ranking formulas) developed by Google, as well as Yahoo, Bing and other search engines. Each search engine has its own proprietary, top-secret algorithm, which is tweaked and changed constantly in order to maintain relevance and to prevent people from abusing the system. In addition, search engines are always trying to improve their products to deliver timely search results that are most relevant to the person searching. Without happy users, the search engines themselves can become irrelevant (remember Ask Jeeves?). All this tweaking and changing of formulas means even if your site is ranking well today, it could change dramatically with the introduction of a big algorithm update. You may have heard of "Panda" or "Penguin"; these refer to updates Google made to its algorithm in past years.

Dozens of factors influence the formulas that determine what website will garner a number 1 ranking for a specific keyword or phrase. Not all of these factors are the same (or carry the same amount of weight) between different search engines. You may be surprised to find out that not only is there no shortcut to optimize your website, there is a fair amount of conjecture and experimentation involved in SEO.

But here is the good news. While search engines are ever-changing and highly intricate, you don't have to be a computer genius to understand the general concepts and apply them to your website. Further, there are many SEO techniques you can do yourself. (You may need the help of a web developer for some of the more technical aspects.)

Green Thumb SEO vs. Sore Thumb SEO*

Your website needs to be search engine friendly, but you should avoid getting carried away trying to optimize your website for robots. It is possible to over-optimize your website, which will be obvious to Google that you are not truly earning your high rankings.

I like to classify SEO techniques into two broad categories: "green thumb SEO," techniques that search engines recommend, and "sore thumb SEO," techniques search engines discourage.

Green thumb SEO tends to produce results that last, whereas sore thumb SEO may get a website penalized or even banned permanently once the search engines discover what they are doing.

When applying Search Engine Optimization techniques, if you are not sure which is which, consider your intentions. If what you are doing is going to be useful to a user on your website, then it is probably green thumb SEO, which means it will help your website thrive and assist in your SEO efforts. If what you are doing is solely to help your rankings, it will likely stick out like a sore thumb to the search engines and to users, and thus, it is probably something you should not be doing.

Above all, you must remember that humans are the ones who will actually drive your business to success. If you follow the guidelines laid out in this book, while focusing on the usability and purpose of your website as it provides real value to real humans, you can sport your green thumb and always remain on the good side of the search engines.

Measuring Progress with Google Analytics

There are many tools and resources available to help in your SEO efforts. I will introduce several in this book, some of which are free and some of which are paid. I won't be getting into precisely how to use each of the tools, but you should be aware of them as you get more serious with your SEO.

Google Analytics is one of the most essential tools you need to measure and track your SEO efforts. Google Analytics is an industry standard tool, and it is free! Until you know what to look for, avoid using other statistics programs offered by your website host or CMS as these may have inflated or inaccurate numbers.

Resource: To sign up for Google Analytics, visit www.google.com/analytics.

You may need a web developer to help you install the Google Analytics code on your website, but it should not be difficult or expensive for them to do. Whatever you do, don't skip this important step! Start tracking your results and progress immediately. These metrics will help you better understand and track your return on investment.

Once the code is installed on your site, you can see exactly how many people are accessing your website, from what parts of the world, at what time of day, what pages they are visiting, for how long and so much more. Warning: once you start tracking, you may find yourself addicted to looking at your analytics. It's incredibly interesting and often surprising!

There is so much data collected it may seem overwhelming to wade through. But at the very least, start tracking the information, and you can always hire an analyst or SEO expert to help you make sense of it later.

***Author's Note:** The SEO industry has classified good and bad SEO techniques as "white hat SEO" and "black hat SEO." I find these terms insensitive to people of color and have purposely omitted them from my book. I call on you to adopt "green thumb SEO" and "sore thumb SEO" as the new industry standard.*

CHAPTER 2

ANATOMY OF A SEARCH ENGINE RESULTS PAGE

The SERP

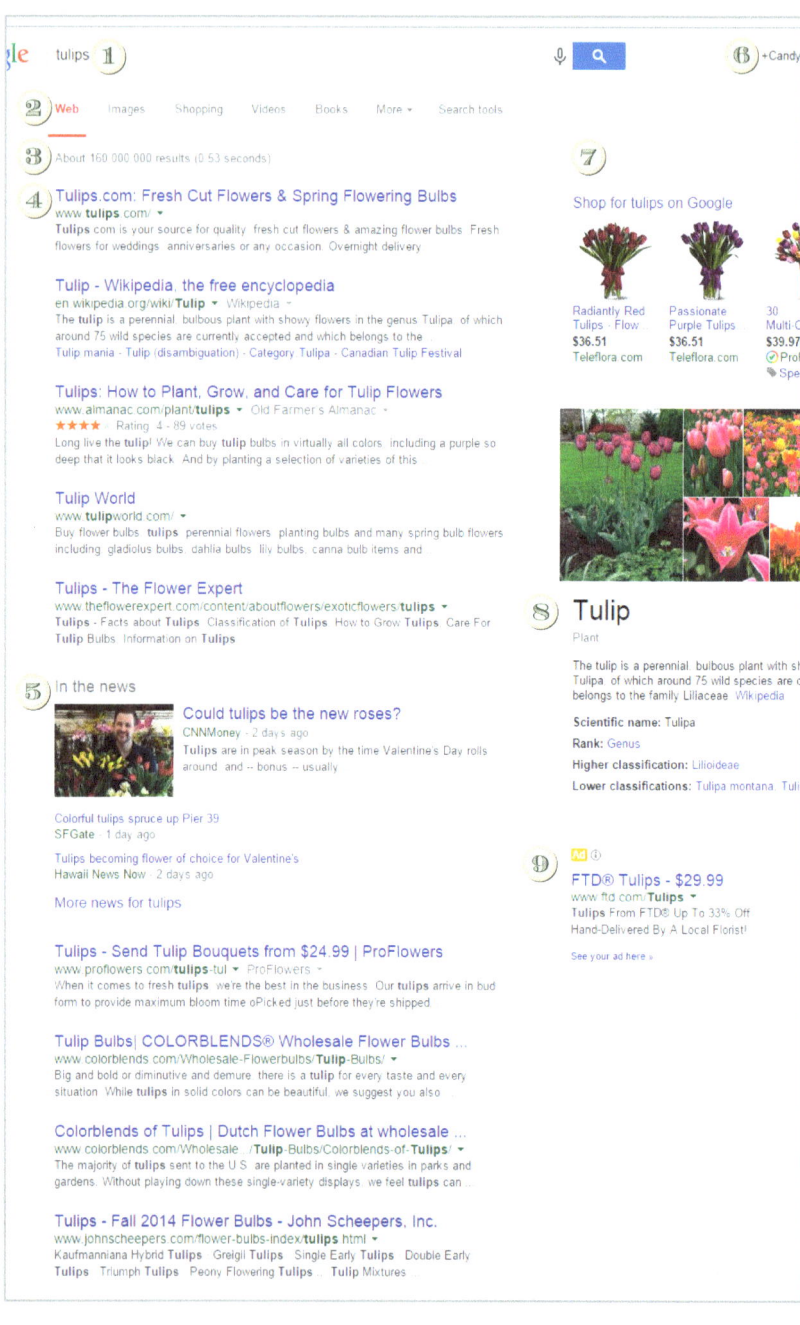

Figure A: A Search Engine Results Page (SERP) from Google.com.

S earch engines are constantly scanning and indexing millions of websites and evaluating countless factors to calculate the most relevant websites to return for the specific keywords for which a user is searching.

A keyword could be a single word: "tulips," a phrase: "world's best tulips," or an entire question: "What are the best conditions for growing tulips?"

When returning results on a SERP, search engines factor in the "relevance" and "authority" of each website to determine which sites are the most helpful and useful for the searcher. In an attempt to provide the most relevant results, the exact same search by different users may result in different SERPs, depending on the type of query. SERPs are tailored specifically for each user based their unique browsing history, location, social media activity and more.

Figure A is an example of a SERP on Google for the keyword "tulips":

1. This is the Search Box. It's where the user types in a keyword, keyword phrase or question.

2. These are different types of searches you can perform on *Google.com*. The web is the default, but you can also search by keyword for images, products, videos, books, news and more. Some SERPs, like this one, will automatically show you a combination.

3. This shows the number of pages indexed by Google that match your keyword search. If your search is very general (such as "tulips") you will get more pages of results than if you type something very specific. Of course, probably no one in the history of the Internet has ever paged through these to see the last page of results when there are thousands of pages of results. Most users stick to the first page of results, which is why your goal as a search engine optimizer should be to get on the first page of results. If users aren't finding what they are looking for, instead of continuing to page through dozens of SERPs, they are more likely to refine their search phrase to make it more specific or better match their intention.

4. On this particular SERP, the top result is an "organic" search result. This means that it is an earned ranking, rather than a paid advertisement. Studies show that users click on organic results over paid ads about 9 times out of 10.

5. Some search results will have reviews, videos, photos and more. This SERP is also showing news articles related to our query.

6. Because I am logged into a Google product, in this case through Gmail, Google knows who I am, where I am and my past search history. This means I will get a customized SERP that may be totally different than what you would receive for the exact same query. As creepy as this is, it can be very helpful.

7. These are displaying the "shopping" search results, which show prices and where you can purchase these products.

8. This "Knowledge Graph Information" is sometimes from third party sources and sometimes from Google's knowledge graph. It is designed to provide answers directly on the SERP, so a user doesn't even have to click on anything to see the information.

9. These are paid advertisements via Google AdWords. You can differentiate these from organic (non-paid, earned) results because of the tiny yellow "ad" icon. Normally, you will also see paid ads at the top of the SERP as well. In this book, we are only talking about SEO for organic search results, not advertising through search engines. But it is important to understand the difference as a user, and as a search engine optimizer, as they can both be valuable.

There are many other types of content you might see on a SERP, depending on various factors.

Resource: For an even more thorough look at all the possibilities, check out the Moz Blog's infographic here: http://moz.com/blog/mega-serp-a-visual-guide-to-google.

CHAPTER **3**

WHY IS SEO SO IMPORTANT?

Inbound Marketing

*H*istorically, websites were a line item in a standard marketing budget, directly beneath the all-important stationery and letterhead expenditures. Websites of yore functioned merely as online versions of the business's brochure, showcasing basic contact information and listing services or products. Business websites used to be optional, and it was very common for businesses to just have a single web page without any additional links. But marketing has evolved!

Traditional "outbound marketing," such as radio, TV and print advertising, are more easily being ignored by shoppers today due to technological advances. People are getting better at blocking out advertising "interruptions." With the proliferation of paperless billing and email, mailboxes contain little mail that people actually want or need and, instead, are chock full of ads. The pile often goes straight from the mailbox into the recycling bin. I know mine does (with the important exception of pizza coupons!) With the advent of Netflix and TiVo, people easily skip over television commercials and previews. With caller ID, telemarketing is no longer as effective. With XM radio and iTunes, radio ads reach fewer people.

This phenomenon—along with other technical advances, social media, and the sheer abundance of information on the web—has spawned a gradual, but powerful, revolution in marketing. These days, shopping doesn't start at the department store; it starts on the web. Shoppers have gone from being passive, semi-brainwashed "advertisees" to being hyper-informed buyers. This new variety of shopper spends time gathering information and reading blogs, turning to social media to ask peers for recommendations, and performing extensive online research using search engines before making decisions on how to spend their money.

According to ComScore, Americans conducted over 13 billion Google searches just in April, 2009[4]. While some of these searches are devoted to discovering the latest adorable-kitten-playing-a-piano video, the vast majority of these queries are steps in a sales cycle that is happening almost entirely online.

Savvy businesses can reach these new age shoppers with "inbound marketing". Inbound marketing refers to marketing activities that bring visitors in, rather than businesses having to go out to get the attention of potential customers. Businesses are pulling people into their sales funnel, rather than pushing them. Inbound marketing includes promoting your website and business through blogs, podcasts, video, eBooks, whitepapers, SEO, social media and other forms of "content marketing." We'll discuss content marketing more in Chapter 5.

Resource: For an even more thorough understanding of inbound marketing, visit www.hubspot.com/inbound-marketing.

A New World of Marketing

The specific keywords a person uses to search can reveal intentions. Think about the difference between the two searches "buy tulips" and "how to plant tulips." One person is shopping, the other needs gardening tips.

Keywords can tell us what actions users are likely to take in that specific moment in time. In the past, this type of information was only attainable by expensive market research studies. By knowing what the user is looking for, businesses can create content that meets their needs, precisely at the moment that they need it. In order to take advantage of this new reality, businesses need to change the way they think about marketing.[5]

With SEO, there is no magic bullet to get the coveted top rank on Google. You have to earn it!

Today, if your business doesn't have a website, it might as well not exist to the millions of people using search engines to find products and services.

Your website should be the center of your marketing efforts, where you drive traffic by providing valuable content to your audience. The more remarkable your content, the more likely it will be seen.

With SEO, there is no magic bullet to get the coveted top rank on Google. You have to earn it! If you are willing to put in some serious sweat equity, you don't need a big budget to see amazing results. (On second thought, if you're getting really sweaty while optimizing your website, you might be doing something wrong).

But if you don't have time to devote to your SEO, you will need to outsource the work, and this could be a significant ongoing investment. The amount of work or investment totally depends on how competitive your industry is and what keywords and locations you are targeting.

This new online "meritocracy" levels the playing field (at least a little bit) between large corporations and small businesses. Unlike many old school marketing strategies, SEO is not as simple as just investing a lot of money and getting immediate success.

More good news for small businesses is that free and inexpensive resources exist to help you on your SEO journey. Armed with a little knowledge, the right tools and good intentions, even the smallest businesses have what it takes to see SEO results. Let's get started!

CHAPTER 4

GRANDMAS, GARDENING & SEO?

The Garden Metaphor

B *ecause the technology behind search engine algorithms is so complex and ever changing, I wanted to find a better way to explain the basic concepts to marketers, business owners and nonprofits in a way that is memorable and easy to understand. Introducing...the garden metaphor. This metaphor helps explain some of the major factors in search engine ranking. I like to joke that this should be easy enough for your grandmother to understand (although it's certainly possible your grandmother is more tech savvy than me!)*

In addition to making for stimulating inter-generational Thanksgiving dinner conversation, I hope this metaphor will also come in handy when you are trying to explain the importance of SEO to clients, bosses, employees, investors and other stakeholders in your organization.

For the purpose of this metaphor, we will say the main goal for both the garden and the website is driving visitor traffic (this is a public garden). So let's talk about how websites are like gardens.

On the most basic level, gardens and websites both have content. We'll talk about the different types of content in the next chapter.

No two gardens or websites are the exact same. Even if two different gardens are made up of the same plants and designed in the same fashion, they will have unique characteristics. The same goes for websites.

Gardens and websites are both affected by internal factors and external factors, some of which are beyond your control. For websites, those internal factors are the site's architecture, code, design, the type and amount of content and the actual words used in the content. External factors include the search engines themselves, competitors' websites, user behavior, industry and technological trends, the website hosting server and more.

For a garden, the internal factors are the plants or seeds and the care you provide (water, fertilizer, pruning, etc.) The external factors are soil conditions, weather and climate.

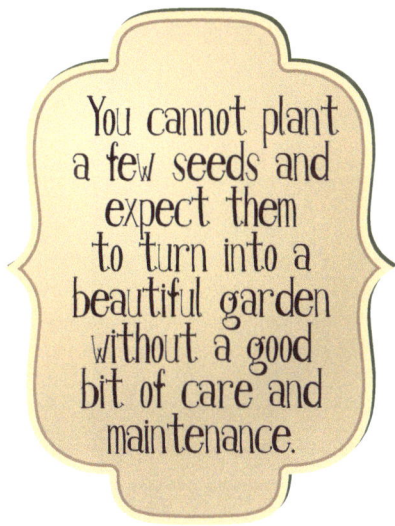

You cannot plant a few seeds and expect them to turn into a beautiful garden without a good bit of care and maintenance.

In both cases, the external factors may be influenced but not controlled.

The most important parallel between gardening and website search engine optimization to understand is this: you must constantly invest time, money or both in order to continue driving traffic. You cannot plant a few seeds and expect them to turn into a beautiful garden that people will want to visit without a good bit of care and maintenance. Likewise, you cannot build a website and expect it to fare well in search engine results without ongoing effort.

This book is for people who are just being introduced to the concepts of SEO. When you start getting into the more advanced search engine optimization (things like canonical page URLs, duplicate content and permalinks), this metaphor may not work as well.

While the metaphor may not hold up 100%, I hope it makes these technical concepts easier to digest.

CHAPTER 5

QUANTITY + QUALITY IS CRITICAL

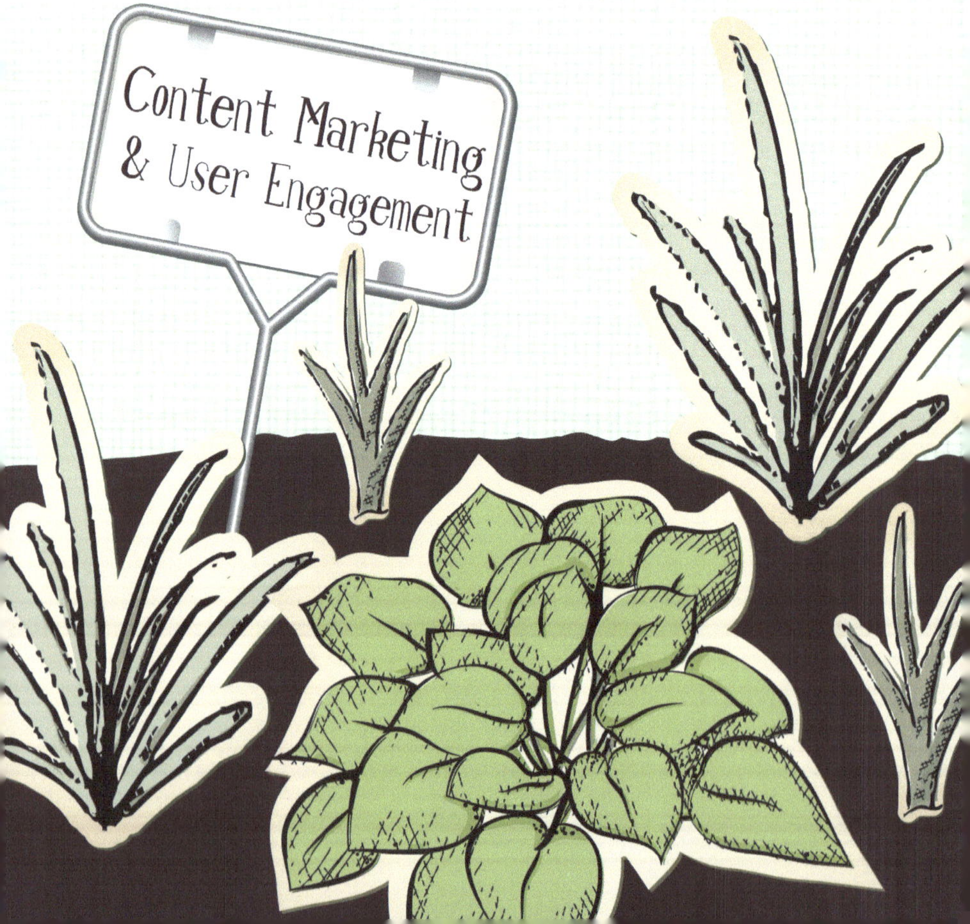
Content Marketing
& User Engagement

A website with only four pages of content is like a garden with only four plants. *The goal must always be to consistently create an abundance of high quality content to drive visitors and keep them engaged for as long as possible.*

Gardens are made up of a wide variety of vegetation and other materials, which I will call "content." The vegetation might contain a combination of flowers, plants, shrubs, trees and grass. The other elements might be rocks, bricks, gravel paths, fencing, etc. The more variety you showcase, the more people will enjoy it.

On a website, content includes text, videos, graphics, photos, animation, buttons, navigation elements and so on. **The number one thing you can do to improve your SEO is to develop high quality content for your website.**

Quantity

Wikipedia.org website contains nearly 35 million pages of content! Obviously this is an extreme example to point out that you need content on your website. Lots of it! The more pages, the better. A website that has dozens of pages of good content will rank higher than a 5-page site if all other factors are the same. A 5-page site will rank higher than a 1-page site. This is why simple "landing pages" with nothing but basic contact information are largely obsolete. With hardly any content or text on the page, you might not even be able to rank on the first page of Google when someone local searches for your business name! That is the ultimate failure in search engine optimization.

One way to get more content is to reorganize, expand

and optimize what you already have. Let's say you are selling 10 different types of vegetable seeds on your site. You could compile all 10 types of the seeds on one long page. There is nothing wrong with this. But for SEO, it would be better to have a page for each type of seed. In addition, you should have a page displaying all 10 varieties with links to individual pages (carrot seeds, cucumber seeds and so on). So for example, you might have a small picture of carrot seeds with the words "carrot seeds" underneath. Both the photo and text link to a page like *www.yourgardensite.com/carrot-seeds*. This multi-page setup gives you more opportunities to optimize each page for one specific type of seed. The carrot page will be more likely to rank when someone Googles "carrot seeds" than a page that has all 10 types of seeds on it.

Quality

Having a lot of content is important, but it's not enough. It must also be quality content. Your garden should be made up of healthy plants that are well cared for. No one wants to walk through a garden totally overgrown with weeds or full of wilting plants. And no one wants to go to a place that boasts a butterfly garden to show up and discover there are no butterflies.

Your website pages should be well written and have substantial quality content that people actually want to read or consume. If your content is helpful, newsworthy, complete, interesting, original or entertaining, people are more likely to spend time reading or consuming your content. Using visual elements and videos will please your visitors, while cramming your content full of ads will annoy them.

Google "Panda" refers to the algorithm changes that

(among other things) helped weed out websites with low-quality content. The most notably affected websites were ones with lots of ads along with weak article content. An example of weak content would be if your headline and on-page SEO indicate the page is about "The Top 5 Lawn Mowers of 2015" but the page actually just contains links to a bunch of lawnmower websites or ads and no actual reviews of lawnmowers. An example of great content is one that advertises "The Top 5 Lawn Mowers of 2015" and actually provides a detailed review of each of the top five lawn mowers with product specs, pricing, photos and links on where to find more information.

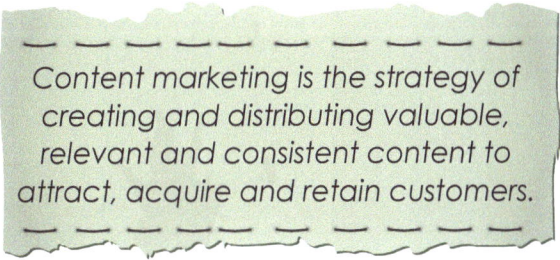

Content marketing is the strategy of creating and distributing valuable, relevant and consistent content to attract, acquire and retain customers.

"Content marketing" is a marketing technique of creating and distributing valuable and relevant content to attract, acquire and retain customers. Instead of pitching your products or services, you provide information that helps your visitors in some way. At the heart of this marketing strategy is the idea that if your business supplies consistent, ongoing valuable information to buyers, they will ultimately reward you with their business and loyalty.

Blogging

The best opportunity a business owner has to create and add content to their website—without having to be a website code ninja— is by using a Content Management

System (CMS) to add content in a blog format. Examples of CMS's are WordPress, Joomla, Drupal or Expression Engine.

If adding a blog to your website is going to help your SEO, it needs to actually "live" on your website (not on *BlogSpot.com, Blogger.com* or the like). Much like a street address, a URL (Uniform Resource Locator) is like a unique address on the Internet telling people where to find a specific page. The URL of your blog should be something like: *www.yourdomain.com/blog*. When users visit your blog, they should be on your website, not on an external site. You don't want the URL of your blog to be something like: *www.yourblog.blogger.com*. This setup drives traffic and backlinks to *www.blogger.com* not *www.yourdomain.com*.

The best type of blog topics are ones your customers will care about and that include keywords that prospective customers will be searching for on Google, Bing and Yahoo. Identify your target audience, as well as what type of "persona" you are trying to attract. Then write articles and create content that you think would appeal to them.

Writing your thoughts or content around a topic that you have seen elsewhere is great. It's fine to link to or reference another piece of content from your blog, so long as it's interesting and high quality. But to maximize your SEO efforts, you want to make sure you're mostly creating original content. I recommend your website should contain at least 75% original content, with 25% coming from syndicated content, article sharing, guest blogging or other sources.

Freshness

If writing a blog isn't in your wheelhouse, then adding

any other type of fresh content to your website is still helpful for your SEO. Keep your website up to date. That could include updating photos or information on the home page, adding new products, a photo gallery, more pages of detailed service or capabilities descriptions, a glossary of industry terms and regularly adding to your frequently asked questions. This is not an exhaustive list; almost any type of new, relevant content will help your Google ranking. Important note: When you add new content, be sure to share it—with a link—on Twitter, Facebook, Google+ and any other social media platforms you maintain. It will be indexed by the search engines that much more quickly.

The more frequently you blog or add new content to your website, the better. Just like when you are gardening, if you continue to plant new seeds or bulbs every month, your garden will continue to expand and flourish. If you plant new seeds every week, your garden will grow that much faster. And as some of the plants mature, you will start to reap the fruits of your labor.

Never copy and paste an article (or other content) from some other website and put it on your site without permission and proper credit. You will get penalized by Google for "scraping" content from someone else's website. Not to mention, you could also introduce legal issues from stealing content if the original author discovers it.

25 Blog Ideas:
High Quality Content for Your Website

———◦———

1. How-to articles (these can be quick how-to's or longer how-to's broken into a series or articles)

2. How-to videos or screencasts

3. Frequently asked questions with detailed explanations

4. Vocabulary or terminology explanations (you can reference these or link to them in other articles or from your email communications)

5. Announcements of upcoming events such as tradeshows, training events, speaking engagements, conferences, etc.

6. Personnel highlights or interviews with staff and management

7. Announcements of work anniversaries or milestones from your company ("we just reached 1,000 customers" or "we are celebrating 10 years in business")

8. A look back at when you started your business and how it has evolved

9) Explanation of your business core values

10) Analysis, summaries or takeaways of past events or trainings

11) Feedback, reviews or synopses of articles or books you read in print publications (make sure to properly credit the original author)

12) Opinion articles or reviews about industry trends or news

13) Case studies of projects you have worked on with anecdotes of lessons learned and project takeaways

14) Interviews with your clients (link to their website so they might link back or share your content)

15) Product reviews or product comparisons

16) Infographics explaining interesting or relevant topics

17) Top 10 thought leaders in your industry you admire (link to their website so they might link back or share your content)

18) Top 10 favorite projects of the year with a short synopsis of each

19) Upcoming industry trend predictions

20 A look at what has changed in your industry since a specific year

21 Descriptions of your perfect customer personas

22 Talk about why what you do is important

23 Top 5 essential tools and resources for your industry or business

24 Top 5 tools or resources for your audience to use

25 Guest blog articles written by people with overlapping interests (these could be from customers, professors, overlapping industries, even competitors or industry peers)

Blogging Bonuses:

Adding quality content to your website will:

- Increase your overall traffic

- Increase the average time spent on your site

- Increase the number of people who find your site through keyword searches on Google

- Decrease your "bounce rate" in your analytics

- Show prospective clients that you are an expert in your field

- Help you beat your competitors in Google page ranking

CHAPTER 6

RELEVANCE IS IMPERATIVE

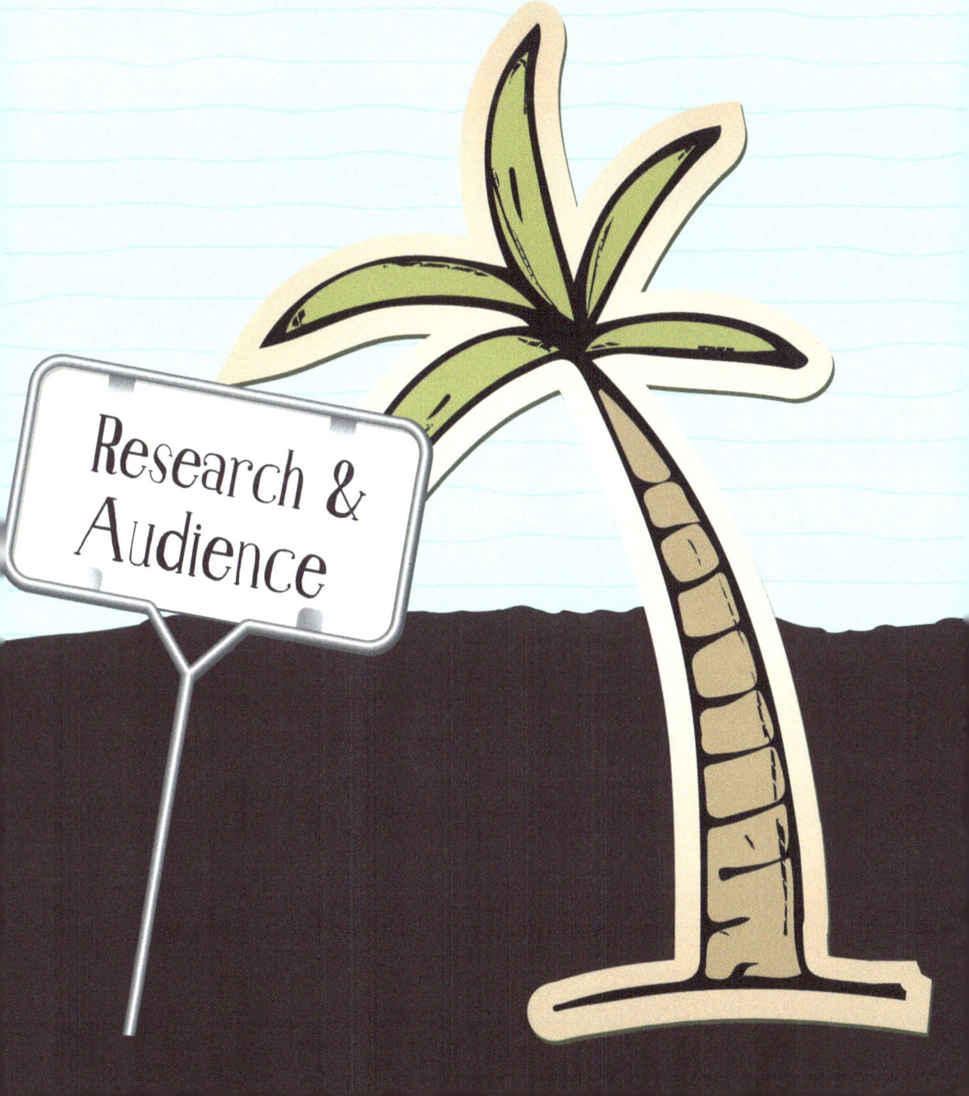
Research &
Audience

*T*here is no sense in planting a palm tree in Wisconsin, just as there is no sense in creating content about Beyoncé on a gardening website. The goal is to provide a wide variety of content while ensuring it is relevant to your audience.

Your garden should contain plants that research shows would be good for climate, light and water conditions for your area. And if you are trying to attract visitors, you should probably plant things that are widely popular, not just row after row of lettuce, (even if you are the world's biggest salad fan).

Your website content should contain researched and relevant keyword phrases that your audience will be using to search for content like yours. The relevance factor is used to determine that a site with information similar to the keywords the searcher uses could also be useful. So someone who searches for a "clay planter" will certainly be able to find websites that sell clay planters. But they will also be served relevant websites that are selling terra-cotta pots. Search engines have complex algorithms that help them sort through all the online information and determine that clay planters and terra-cotta pots are similar. Thus, they assume they would have intersecting relevance for searchers and will show up on SERPs even if the exact words were not used in the search.

The more relevant your content is to the specific query of a searcher, the more likely that person is to stay on your site for a longer period of time and interact. This could be in the form of making a purchase, reading additional articles, clicking around to multiple pages on your site or filling out a contact form. These are all actions that you want the user to take on your website, which prove to Google that the user found your website to be relevant.

The more engagement users have on your website, the higher you will rank.

Keyword Research

In order to find out what keywords might be relevant for your audience, you must perform research. Keyword research is one of the essential tasks of search engine optimization. You need to know what keywords people are typing into the search engines, at what frequency and how relevant those keywords are to you and your business. You also need to know how competitive a specific keyword phrase is.

If you have a website about gardening, you might think trying to rank for a keyword such as "gardening" would be the obvious choice. But after doing keyword research you would probably find out that it is too competitive, meaning it is highly unlikely that you would ever be able to rank on the first or even second page of results. That doesn't mean you shouldn't use the word "gardening" on your website—you definitely should. But you might instead try to optimize your a page on your website for a more specific keyword phrase such as "vegetable gardening tips for beginners." This type of phrase will be much easier to get ranked for.

Understanding which websites already rank for your keyword or keyword phrase can give you valuable insight into the competition and also give you an idea how hard it will be to rank for a given term. Typically, if a keyword search is showing many ads, this indicates it is highly competitive. Multiple search ads above the organic results often indicate a highly lucrative and directly conversion-prone keyword such as "buy tulips".

One way to evaluate the competition of a specific keyword is to examine the Pay Per Click (PPC) side of things with Google AdWords. You can see how many people are trying to pay for advertising for a specific keyword and what they are willing to pay for it. If a keyword's AdWords PPC suggested bid is extremely high, you can bet the correlating organic keyword will also be very competitive.

Do a Google search and see what comes up. Obviously, if you are competing with Amazon or Home Depot for a keyword, it may be virtually impossible for your small business or organization to outrank these behemoths.

But often, local searches are highly attainable for small businesses. Instead of trying to rank for "tulips" on a national level, you might want to just start with targeting local searchers who type in "tulips Madison."

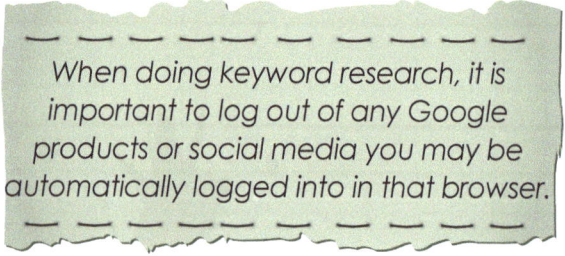

When doing keyword research, it is important to log out of any Google products or social media you may be automatically logged into in that browser.

When doing keyword research like this, it is important to log out of any Google products or social media you may be automatically logged into in that browser. It is also a good idea to clear your web browsing history, or better yet, use a different computer altogether.

If you are logged in to various accounts, or if you have prior history of visiting certain sites, this will skew the results that show on the SERP. Notably, a site that you have visited before (i.e. your own) will often get ranked higher for you than for someone who has never before been there. This can make you think you are ranking better than you really are.

 Resource: To perform keyword research, we recommend setting up a Google AdWords account and using their Keyword Planning Tool: https://adwords.google. com/KeywordPlanner

---

The Google Keyword Planning Tool suggests alternative keyword phrases, estimates traffic and even tells you how much you would need to bid to place an ad for that keyword. It's a great idea to run a few test AdWords campaigns to help figure out the best verbiage for your organic strategy.

Once you have identified a large list of keyword phrases to use for your website, you will want to select 5 or 6 to start with. If you try to optimize your website for too many different keyword phrases at one time, you will spread your efforts too thin and struggle to get good results. Start with the "low hanging fruit" keyword phrases. In other words, start with phrases that are not highly competitive. Once you start ranking on the first page for some of those keyword phrases, then you can leverage your momentum to go for more competitive keywords or keyword phrases.

Once you have your short list of keyword phrases, you might be wondering what you are supposed to be doing on your website to optimize it. The most important action to take at this point is to create content around those keywords.

When writing and creating content, use terminology laypeople would use (assuming of course that your customers are laypeople), including "long-tail keyword phrases" in titles and headings. Long-tail phrases are those that are longer than just 2 or 3 keywords and often contain questions such as "how do I…?" "what is the best…?" or "why is it important to…?" Long-tail phrases are easier to rank for, and people searching by specific "long-tail" phrases are often further down the sales funnel and therefore may be easier to convert into paying customers.

The placement of keywords on a web page is one factor in on-site SEO. Search engines (and of course humans!) want to know quickly whether the content on the page is what they are looking for, which is why it is important to use keywords in page titles, page headings and page URLs. You want to use the same keyword phrase at least a couple of times in the body text. Use keywords in the text for buttons and hyperlinks (also known as anchor text). So for example, instead of something generic like "Click here!" your button or link text might say "Buy Tulips Now!"

Keep your writing natural, and use keywords only as it makes sense to do so. In other words, don't over-optimize a page to the point it looks obvious to a user of your website. An example of an over-optimized headline is "Buy Tulips, Purchase Tulips, Order Tulips Online." This headline would never be used in a print advertisement because it doesn't make sense. So avoid "stuffing" keywords like this on your website.

Resource: If you have a WordPress website, we recommend this tool to help determine the right balance of keywords on a single page for SEO. https://wordpress.org/plugins/wordpress-seo

All this research and strategizing can seem

overwhelming. But when all else fails, stay focused on your high level marketing strategy and your audience. When considering relevance in SEO keywords, you must ask yourself whether or not the keyword accurately reflects the nature of your product or services. After all, the point of SEO is to drive qualified leads to your site who may actually become your customers.

It can be tempting to add a giant list of keywords to a single page on your website in order to optimize a page for multiple keywords. This will hurt your SEO. Stick to one keyword phrase per page, write naturally and don't "stuff" keywords. A user should never be able to tell that you are trying to optimize your website.

It's also a bad idea to try to optimize your site for a popular term that has nothing to do with your business (think "Beyoncé photos"). Even if you are tricky enough to get ranked for something that is not relevant to your products or services, eventually you will get penalized for misleading users. And that's not to mention the backlash from the users!

CHAPTER 7

ORGANIZATION IS IMPORTANT

Architecture & Navigation

LETTUCE

HERBS

Y our garden and website should be well planned, organized and easy to get around. The goal is to make it easy for people to find what they are looking for.

In a garden, grouping related plants (i.e. herbs) in one area makes it easy for people to find what interests them. Providing maps and signage is also helpful. Using labels on plants helps people understand what they are looking at.

Similarly, your website should be organized and easy to navigate. One thing to consider is the structure and overall page layout of the site. Search engines—just like people— want it to be obvious what pages are on the site and how they are related to each other. Through internal linking in a navigation system, you show users and search engines the structure of your site. The navigation should be intuitive and make logical sense to users and search engines alike.

If you have a blog, it should be organized into topical categories with more specific subjects identified by "tags," which help people to sort information and find related material. Try to use keywords in both the category names and the tags. For example, a category might be "native plants," and a tag might be "prairie dropseed."

One thing that will infuriate users and hurt your SEO is having broken links or missing pages. It would be like having a sign in your garden that says "Herb Garden This Way" that actually directs visitors to an empty field.

If a link is broken, a user will get the all-too-ubiquitous 404 error, a page saying the URL you tried to find does not exist. At the very least you should have a 404 page template so when a user gets a broken or missing link, a user can easily get to another page on your website by using the navigation menu. If a page has disappeared because the URL has changed, it's a good idea to have your web developer add a 301 redirect to the new page.

 Resource: We recommend installing a tool such as Broken Link Checker on your WordPress website https://wordpress.org/plugins/broken-link-checker. This will show you if you have broken links so you can remedy them.

It's a great idea to have an onsite search box so someone can type in a word or phrase and quickly find out if your site has that content. This can also provide clues as to whether people are able to find what they are looking for using your navigation.

Advanced SEO Topics

In gardening, there are a few things for which a novice gardeners would likely need to seek professional help. For example, you would not try to use a tractor to re-grade a large area of soil or build a 6-foot retaining wall if you didn't know what you were doing.

With SEO, there are also a few things that affect your Google ranking but are more complex than an average business owner or marketer would want to learn about.

There are many important elements in the code of a website that make up its architecture that will either facilitate or encumber the ability for search engines crawling your site. When building the website, your developer should be using SEO best practices to ensure your site is easy for search engines to index.

The topics below are important for SEO but beyond the scope of this book. I am listing them so you are aware they are factors, but I will not go into details or definitions.

- the use of "divs" instead of tables for layout
- dynamic sitemaps
- appropriate placement of scripts and other code
- meaningful URLs (otherwise known as "pretty permalinks")
- duplicate content issues (often a result of on-site search pages or archive pages)
- and schema markup.

Resource: To read more about some of these complex SEO topics, we recommend this book: www.amazon. com/Inbound-Marketing-SEO-Insights-Blog/ dp/1118551559

If your web developer plans to use a proprietary CMS (i.e. one they created that is not "open source"), ask him or her about SEO before committing to any contracts. You are safer sticking to one of the major CMS's, such as WordPress, Joomla, Drupal and Expression Engine. These are already built with SEO best practices and updated regularly.

Sore Thumb SEO

You should never have content or pages that are visible to search engines but hidden from real people.

CHAPTER 8

GOOD DESIGN GETS YOU FAR

Design & Audio Visual Content

Your garden and website should be well designed and full of beautiful and stimulating content. Your website's template is like your overall garden blueprint; your visual content is like individual plants or specific types of gardens within the larger garden. The goal is to maximize engagement and delight visitors.

Using the proper spacing, hierarchy, symmetry, scale, color contrast, etc. in gardening will make for a visually pleasing garden design. Even a single unique plant or tree used as a focal point will attract visitors from miles around. Also don't forget to consider the other aspects of plants that make them engaging, (things like fragrance, texture and edibility).

Your website should be designed by a professional using design best practices. Like in your garden, many of the same design rules apply to building your site: spacing, hierarchy, symmetry, scale and color contrast. Good design builds trust and increases the perceived value of a product or service. Bad design may turn people off, hinder readability or cause confusion or suspicion. Even if you have the latest and greatest information about hydroponic gardening on your website, if it looks like it was designed in 1994, people will not believe that you have current or reliable content. Naturally, they will quickly move on to the next website.

If you plan to build your own website, use a CMS like WordPress that has customizable templates designed by professionals. Some of the drag-and-drop site builder tools offered by Vista Print or GoDaddy might be easy to use, but often they result in awkward looking (or plain old ugly) designs. If you don't have the "design eye" and can't tell if what you are building looks good or bad, model your website after other professionally built sites or have friends and family give you a friendly critique.

 Resource: A great place to find beautifully designed WordPress templates is Theme Forest: http://themeforest.net.

You want the design of your website to match your other marketing materials. This is important for branding as well as building trust. You website should use the same colors, imagery, design style and graphics to match as closely as possible. Fonts may be the exception to this rule.

Fonts on the Web

There are many limitations to using fonts on the Internet because most fonts are proprietary and have strict licensing agreements. Internet browsers (i.e. Chrome, Internet Explorer and Firefox) interpret code to display web pages to people. If you use a font on your website that the end user does not have installed on their computer or device, the browser can't display that text. Thus, designers are restricted to using only very common "web-friendly" fonts, such as Arial, Helvetica and Times New Roman. Nearly everyone has these basic fonts installed.

Another option is to use something called "hosted fonts." These are collections of fonts made available by the designers/founders for use (free or paid) by website developers. The fonts reside on the Internet and thus are available for nearly any computer or device to display "live" text.

Resource: To find free hosted fonts
you can use on your website, check
out www.google.com/fonts. To find
additional hosted fonts available in a paid
subscription, check out https://typekit.com.

In order to get around this font limitation, some designers will embed text in images so they can use a specific font that may not be available on the web. This strategy can make for a very visually pleasing, unique website that is quick and easy to build. However, many business owners and novice web designers don't understand the negative impact this has on their SEO.

> *You want the vast majority of text on your website to be "live" text rather than text embedded in images. Image-based text is readable only to humans, not search engines.*

You want the vast majority of text on your website to be "live" text, not text embedded in images. Image-based text is readable only to humans, not search engines. Thus if you have a site where the navigation and headlines are all image-based, you are missing some of the most important areas for live text keywords on your website. Hint: If you can't tell if text is live text or embedded in an image, try to copy and paste the text into a text editor. If you can't highlight, copy and paste it, it is probably part of an image.

Visual Content

Images and graphics are a must on every website and blog! Having a website without visual elements is like having a garden that is made up entirely of grass. Sure everyone loves a nice lawn, but it's really not that interesting in and of itself. Your website could have the greatest text content in the world, but if it has no images, people will likely not read it.

Non-text content is essential for user engagement. It communicates in a different way than written content and naturally motivates people to interact with it.

Images can be used to break up text, to illustrate a point, to add visual explanations, to delight and more. Using images of real people who work at your business or organization can build trust a lot more effectively than the ubiquitous lady-with-a-headset stock photo. Customers like knowing there are real people behind the website. The best images are professional photos of your business, you and your staff, your products and your services in action. Hiring a professional to take photos is a wise investment.

 Resource: If you don't have any images of your own, we recommend stock photo websites such as www.dreamstime.com or www.shutterstock.com to find high quality images. Stock photos are always better than no photos!

Highlighting visual and multi-media elements often makes content easier or more entertaining to consume. Visual content can include photographs, graphics, animations, illustrations and infographics. Multi-media content (audio and video) have proven to dramatically aid in SEO. Many users are far more likely to watch a five-minute video than they are to read an article for five minutes. The longer users remain on your site and engage, the better your Google ranking will be. In one study of 600 marketers, 82% surveyed confirmed that online video marketing has had a positive impact on their organization or business. Just 10% felt video has had little impact on their overall marketing ROI with 7% confirming they had not yet integrated video into their marketing programs.[6]

Design & Readability

In addition to being pleasing to the eye, good design will help users consume and understand information more easily. To make a big block of text easier to read, add subheadings to break up text and introduce new topics. Headlines should follow a hierarchy, with the most important headline being the largest text on the page. This allows people to quickly scan and find what they are looking for and identify what the most important things are to read.

In the body text, make sure there is extra vertical space after paragraphs (more space than between sentences in the same paragraph) to visually separate each paragraph.

In addition, use short bullets and numbered lists whenever possible. For example, instead of writing one big block of text about your favorite flowers, write "My Top 10 Favorite Flowers" and break up the article with subheadings and numbers for each flower. That way, someone who may not want to read the entire article can quickly see what the top 10 flowers are.

Make sure the font size is easy to read and the contrast between the text color and the background color is high enough that your eyes don't have to strain.

Designing with large buttons, arrows, images and other graphics can drive viewers to take a specific action much like signage and a path in a garden can direct people to a specific place. Design can help dictate the flow a user takes through your website: to complete a contact form, download an e-book, purchase a product or the like. If the verb used is a command, this type of element is known as a "call to action." "Buy Now," "Click Here" and "Download Your Free Resource" are all examples of calls to action.

Highlighting visual and multi-media elements often makes content easier or more entertaining to consume.

Responsive Design

Design plays a major role in SEO when it comes to the latest technology. The vast array of Internet-connected devices (things like smart phones, smart watches and Google glasses) and the infinite number of screen sizes on everything from tiny tablets, to jumbo computer monitors create significant challenges for web designers. With all the different ways your site might be viewed, web designers have had to change tactics to create websites that will meet the needs of users on all of these different types of devices (or at least to provide them with an experience that isn't terrible). Enter "responsive design."

Responsive web design is the approach in design and development wherein the website responds to the user's behavior and environment based on screen size, platform and orientation. Responsive design is created by using a mix of flexible grids, layouts and images. A responsive web design will dynamically optimize itself for phones and tablets, as the of size screen on which it's being displayed changes.

A responsive website is different than a mobile app because you don't have separate mobile, tablet and desktop versions of your site. Regardless of what device a visitor is using to access your site, they'll see all of the content you have to offer (no more partial-content mobile versions of sites) and they'll encounter it in an easy-to-read format (See Figure B).

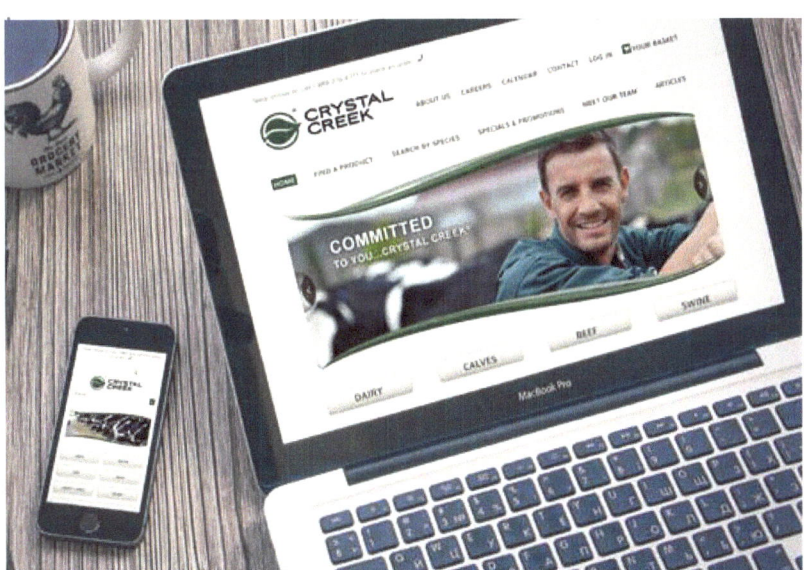

Figure B: A responsive website shown on a laptop and a mobile phone.

With mobile use on the rise, user experience on these various devices is more important than ever. Buttons must be large enough to be easily clicked with a finger without touching another link or button. Important content must be accessible without having to pinch and zoom or scroll sideways. Designs must work on dozens of different sized monitors, some as small as a dollar bill, others the size of a huge TV. Responsive design is the answer to this challenge. We will look at responsive design more in the next chapter.

The better optimized your site is for all these different devices, the higher user engagement you will have. When users stay on your website for longer periods of time, click to multiple pages and ultimately take the action you want them to take, Google will reward you.

Invest in a website that is interesting to look at and easy for people to use, and it will definitely pay off. While form may not trump function, there's no question that design plays a vital role in user experience, engagement, perceived value, readability, trust building and your search engine optimization.

Sore Thumb SEO

It is possible to hide content on a website by making the text the same color as the background in order to show content to search engines but not humans. Google's robots are smart enough to detect this, and you will be penalized for it!

CHAPTER 9

EASY ACCESS IS CRUCIAL

Speed &
Accessibility

*E*ven if you have a magnificent garden or website, if it is difficult for visitors to access, your traffic count will suffer. The goal should be to make your garden and website easy to access for everyone.

If there is limited parking and a 20-minute wait time to enter your garden, many people will simply leave. If you make it difficult for people with wheelchairs or strollers to get around, those who enter won't want to stay. You should attempt to eliminate barriers to make the garden easy to access for everyone. However, keep in mind there are always going to be exceptions and compromises. For example, if someone wants to drive through your garden in a horse-drawn carriage, you should not redesign your entire garden to accommodate the carriage (unless of course you expect a lot of horse-drawn carriage traffic).

Site Speed

Page load time is a user experience issue that must not be overlooked. Your website should load quickly (within a few seconds), or most people won't stick around long enough to see the content, no matter how good it might be. Some things that can negatively affect your site load time are the following:

- using too many WordPress plug-ins

- improperly placed scripts

- poorly written or broken code

- using more than one hosted font

- an overloaded shared web hosting server

- a layout built with html "tables"

- and photos that aren't optimized for the web.

The good news is that very few people still use dial-up Internet. But with the dramatic increase in mobile use, many people are accessing websites on the go from less-than-lightning-speed connections. As of the past few years, Google is factoring site speed into its page ranking formula. The faster your site, the better.

Resource: You can test your page load time here: http://gtmetrix.com

Sometimes you might have to make tough decisions when it comes to page load time and accessibility. Compromises will have to be made. For example, having a large slideshow on your home page will cause the load time to lag for slow Internet connections, but you may determine that it is worth it to have beautiful photos because they load quickly for most of your users, who use high-speed Internet. You may decide to use a specific feature on your site even though you know it isn't supported in an older browser such as Internet Explorer 6. If the feature adds so much value in terms of function or design for the people who have more up-to-date browsers, you may decide the benefits outweigh losing accessibility for a few people.

Rigorous testing on multiple devices will help you know whether your site has issues of site speed, browser support or accessibility. When faced with an issue, look at your target audience to help determine what you should do. If you are targeting an elderly crowd or people in other countries, you may want to accommodate older browsers. If you are targeting millennials, you will definitely want to accommodate smart phones.

If you have Google Analytics or another traffic tracking program installed on your site, you can see exactly how many people are accessing your website from certain browsers or devices. This may help you make some of those tough decisions.

Accessibility

Websites are made up of "code" (i.e. html and php) which is not readily visible to humans. Some of this code is specifically designed for visually impaired people who use screen reading devices to read the text and certain code on a website aloud. "Alt text" and title meta tags comprise the special code used to describe image content for people using screen readers who can't see the pictures. When uploading a photo or graphic to your website, you can add alt text and a title. When doing so, you should use keywords and descriptions that make sense for that image or page. (Many times you will use the same text for both tags.) For example, if you upload an image of a fern, the alt text and title tag might say "fern plant." If you upload a chart with suggested watering times, the tags might say "Chart displaying a water schedule for fern plants in Wisconsin." It will help your SEO (minimally) to use keywords in these tags, but moreover, it will help people who can't see the images.

The Use of Flash

Once upon a time, developers built websites with Adobe

Flash. Flash (formerly known as Macromedia Flash and Shockwave Flash) is a multimedia and software platform used for creating graphics, animation, games and applications that can be viewed or played in Adobe Flash Player. Flash boasts rich design tools. Developers can create very complex animations and video-like features on a website that enhance interactivity.

However, in recent years, the use of Flash on websites has plummeted, largely because the decision-makers at Apple chose not to support its use on iOS devices such as iPhones and iPads. According to Wikipedia[7]:

> In April 2010, Steve Jobs, the co-founder and chief executive officer of Apple Inc. published an open letter explaining why Apple wouldn't allow Flash on the iPhone, iPod touch and iPad. In the letter he cited the rapid energy consumption, poor performance on mobile devices, abysmal security, lack of touch support, and desire to avoid "a third party layer of software coming between the platform and the developer". He also touched on the idea of Flash being "Open", claiming that "By almost any definition, Flash is a closed system."

A Flash website is not only "not optimized" for phones and tablets, a website built in Flash is not viewable at all on iPhones and iPads. In addition, Flash is not an SEO friendly platform. This is almost an obsolete warning, but it needs to be stated: Be absolute sure that your web developer will not be using Flash to build your website!

Responsive Design & Accessibility

We've already talked about responsive websites in terms

of design. From an accessibility standpoint, responsive design is, once again, the best way to make your site easy to use for mobile and tablet visitors. It is important to test the functionality, page load time and user interface in various browsers and on multiple types of devices. This will ensure an easy and seamless experience for the most users possible.

Choosing a responsive website versus a separate mobile website is a highly debated topic. Both options have pros and cons. Having a separate desktop and mobile site requires having separate content management, SEO, tracking and measuring. In that respect, responsive wins. That being said, there are benefits to having a mobile-specific SEO strategy, such as optimizing for keywords that are more likely to be searched when someone is on their smart phone.

At the end of the day, for SEO purposes, I recommend using responsive design because, well... Google says so.

Google recommends that developers follow the industry best practice of using responsive web design, serving the same HTML for all devices and using only "CSS media queries" to decide the rendering on each device. "Create flexible, not fixed, layouts."

Resource: Keep up with news regarding what Google says about responsive web design here: www.developers.google.com

Until recently, this was just a recommendation. But as of April 2015, Google actually started factoring in mobile friendliness into its algorithm for page rank. When describing the effect these changes will have on mobile SERPs, the Google developers specifically said that there would be a "significant impact on search results" for websites that didn't have a mobile friendly option.

As long as Google is recommending a responsive layout, we would tend to agree. Arguing with Google seems kind of pointless, don't you think?

Do not use alt tags or meta data as an opportunity to "stuff" keywords just because they aren't visible. This was a very early sore thumb SEO technique. Due to its abuse, search engines do not weight meta data and alt tags heavily when factoring in keywords for your website ranking.

CHAPTER 10

LONGEVITY IS AN ADVANTAGE

History & Authority

*B*uilding your garden's reputation as a destination is not something that happens overnight, just as building your website search engine authority takes time. The goal is to stick around in the same place long enough to allow things to develop and to be able to leverage your longevity.

The longer your garden is around, the better it gets. More visitors are likely to go to an established garden that has mature trees and developed plants. No one wants to walk around a garden composed mainly of seedlings and dirt. Once you've planted your seeds, don't move the location of your garden unless it is absolutely necessary. This should be avoidable with proper planning.

Websites that have been around a long time automatically have more authority than brand new websites (all other factors being equal). Websites for government agencies, nonprofits, industry organizations and media outlets also have more automatic authority.

Resource: One way to measure your search engine authority (and your competitors' authority) is at this website: www.alexa.com.

The Internet has over a billion websites, according to *www.Internetlivestats.com*[8]. That's a website for every 7th person on the planet! It is incredible that there is a formula to rank all of them. Out of the billion websites in the world, Wikipedia.org's rank is #6, according to Alexa.

Search engine authority, or credibility, is affected by many things, including the number of external links to your site, the length of time your domain has been registered, the total number of pages indexed for a site and many other variables. Trusted, authoritative websites (as Google sees it) are ones with high traffic and lots of high quality, fresh content.

In addition to following the SEO best practices outlined in this book, you can increase your website's authority by driving more traffic to your site. This means, instead of sitting around hoping people find your site on Google, you should be actively giving your clients, leads, employees, media and others reasons to visit your website. The more traffic you drive to your website, the higher it will rank. The higher it ranks, the more traffic you will get. So you can see how once you get some SEO momentum, you can keep building on it as long as you keep at it.

Like with gardening, you must be prepared to continually work on your search engine optimization. In addition, be prepared for your SEO strategy to take some time to be implemented and to start gaining traction. But once you get some momentum, you can leverage that earned authority to get an even better ranking for more competitive keywords.

Search engines may take days or weeks to react to the new content you add to your website and then to index it appropriately. To speed up the process of your website being indexed, you can register your website with major search engines. Google and Bing have webmaster tools that allow you to submit sitemaps. Make sure your website is being indexed properly using their tools and insights.

 Resource: www.google.com/webmasters and www.bing.com/toolbox/webmaster

15 IDEAS
TO DRIVE NEW AND REPEAT
TRAFFIC TO YOUR WEBSITE

1. Add your website URL to all of your marketing materials (brochures, business cards, stationery, etc.)

2. Mention your URL in all radio or TV ads.

3. Add your website URL to your email signature.

4. Link to your website from your social media posts regularly.

5. Give away special offers on your website like discounts or coupons.

6. Instead of describing products, services, capabilities or Frequently Asked Questions in an email, send links to that information on your website.

7. Give away e-books or white papers on your website with valuable industry information.

8. If you have a questionnaire or form that needs to be filled out, have people fill it out on your website instead of on paper or a PDF.

9 Use a QR code on marketing materials, t-shirts or places around your business and encourage people to scan them with their phones for more information or a special offer. (QR codes are machine-readable code consisting of an array of black and white squares, typically used for storing URLs or other information for reading by the camera on a smartphone.)

10 Accept job applications or requests for charitable donations via forms on your website.

11 Post an event calendar, class schedule or employee schedule on your website.

12 Add special tools, software or features to your website such as a special calculator, estimating system or help forum.

13 If people need to send you files or images, create a form with upload fields on your website.

14 Deliver customer product delivery or service updates on your website instead via emails or phone calls.

15 Provide a download of your high-resolution logo and other branding files needed by designers or media outlets where you are advertising.

Domain Names

You can change your website host at any time, but don't change your website domain unless absolutely necessary. It's best if you pick a flexible domain in case your business changes later. For example, don't buy *redtulips.com* if it is possible that some day you would also be selling yellow tulips or other types of flowers. It's OK to buy multiple domains, but your primary domain name should be something you can use for a long time (hopefully the lifetime of your business or organization).

Of course, like all rules, there are exceptions. For example, let's say you start a business called The Garden Center, and you can't find a domain name that works well because all the good ones are taken. You end up choosing "*yourgarden-centermadison.biz*". This is one of those horrible domains that gives you grief every time you try to tell it to someone over the phone. Some people don't know what a hyphen is, and others type in ".com" even though you tell them it's ".biz." Then five years go by, you're starting to gain some SEO traction, and "*thegardencenter.com*" becomes available. By all means, buy that domain and switch immediately!

You'll want make sure your website developer adds "301 redirects" from your old URLs. But the benefits of having a memorable and easy-to-use domain in this case far outweigh the short-term loss of search engine authority. A 301 redirect is like a note to Google saying "We've moved. Visit us at our new location!" By connecting the old and new domains, you are proving that you have nothing to hide and that the switch was for a legitimate reason.

There is a good reason that the length of time your website has been around is a factor in SEO. Many sore thumb marketers will build websites and drive traffic to them by committing some of the "sore thumb no no's" we've discussed in this book. When they inevitably get discovered and banned from Google's indexes, they reappear as a new website under a new domain and start the Sore Thumb process again. That's why it looks suspicious to search engines to change your domain name frequently, so don't do it unless it's really necessary.

CHAPTER 11

REPUTATION IS EVERYTHING

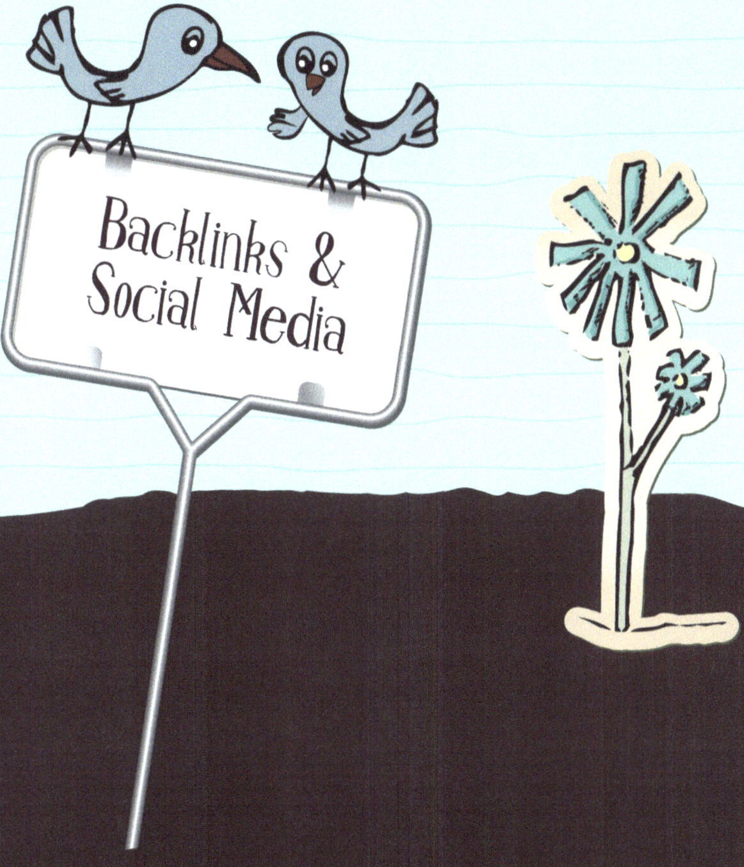

Backlinks &
Social Media

O ld fashioned word-of-mouth recommendations are to your garden what external link building and social media sharing are to your website. The goal is to get as much buzz as possible from as many high profile places as possible.

If your garden is an exciting place to visit, people will recommend it and share their experiences with others. If someone's best friend tells her to visit your garden, that will carry more weight than a stranger's recommendation. However if several strangers recommend a visit to your garden, that may start to pique a person's curiosity.

In SEO, backlinks (also known as inbound links, link-backs, inlinks and inward links) are incoming hyperlinks to your website from an external website. A social share is when someone links to your content from a post or update on their Facebook, Twitter, Linked In, Google Plus or other social media account.

When someone shares your content "socially" or posts a backlink to your website, they are essentially recommending that people check out your site. They might be interested in your entire website (i.e. *This is the best online source of gardening tips I've ever found! Check out www.thegardencenter.com!*"). Or they might backlink or share a specific piece of content on your site ("*Check out this fantastic article about pruning rose bushes! www.thegardencenter.com/blog/rose-pruning*").

The number of backlinks a site garners is one indication of the popularity or importance of that website or page. Thus Google and other search engines use that as one factor in determining the overall page rank of a website. Likewise, the number of people who have shared your content on their social media platforms and the activity generated by those posts are also factors in the ranking algorithm.

Backlink accumulation used to be one of the most important factors in SEO, but it quickly became one of the most abused sore thumb SEO tricks in the book. "Google Penguin" is the algorithm change aimed to weed out websites that have over-optimized on-site and off-site SEO. Link buying and having an "unnatural" link profile are just two of the indicators to Google that a website has attempted to manipulate search rankings.

Google is now pushing businesses and organizations to have legitimate websites with real visitors and to connect with real people through social media channels. Google then rewards this effort by giving those active and popular websites preferential treatment in SERPs.

In general, the more backlinks your site has, the better. But not all backlinks are created equal. A link or social share from an authoritative website or social profile carries more weight than a less authoritative site. Links from brand new websites or sites with very low traffic are not weighted heavily.

In addition, your link building must appear natural. This means inbound links should build slowly over time. A huge spike in the number of backlinks to your website from low quality sites is a red flag that the backlinks aren't earned, but rather paid.

Resource: To check the number of external backlinks your website has, visit https://majestic.com.

So how do you get more good quality backlinks and shares? Of course, it comes back to creating high quality, popular content. However, there are a few additional things you can do. Register your website with the main search engines and directories to get a few crucial backlinks.

Directories exist to help sort and direct web users to businesses much like the good ol' phonebook used to do. In fact, *YP.com* (aka the new Yellow Pages) is one of the largest web directories out there. Once the company leaders realized the phonebook was quickly losing relevance, they jumped on board as a web directory. They even offer SEO as a service! *Manta.com* and *Thumbtack.com* are other directories worth looking into.

You should also look for directories that are specific to your industry, as this will likely help drive traffic to your website in addition to providing a valuable backlink. For example, you might want to register your garden website with a statewide garden club site. Registering for these types of sites is something you can do yourself. Many of these are free, but some are paid. It is up to you to determine whether the paid listings are worth it for your business. Note: paid listings in legitimate directories will not hurt your SEO like paying for backlinks on scam websites and "link farms." Once again, consider the end user. If the directory provides value to users, then a backlink from that website will be good for your SEO. If the website is spammy or provides weak content, it is probably best to avoid being associated with it.

In addition to directories, getting accounts set up on the major social media venues will allow you to distribute your content to reach different audiences. Set up your profile and make absolutely sure to link to your website from your social media accounts. At the very least, fill out your bio information and try to post things at least once a month. If you only have time to manage two or three social media channels, picking which ones to use depends on your business and industry. Go where you

12 Backlink Opportunities

—◦—

1 Google +
www.plus.google.com

2 Yahoo Local
www.listings.local.yahoo.com/overview.php

3 Bing
www.bing.com/businessportal

4 Hot Frog
www.bit.ly/1a7cdvS

5 Facebook
www.facebook.com

6 Pinterest
www.pinterest.com

7 Linked In
www.linkedin.com

8 Twitter
www.twitter.com

9 Manta
www.bit.ly/1Fe8rJo

10 Yelp
www.biz.yelp.com/claiming

11 Angie's List
www.angieslist.com

12 Foursquare
www.bit.ly/1DCU3Qa

will get the most bang for your buck. As a general rule, I recommend Google+, Facebook and Pinterest for B2C (business to consumer) and Google+, Twitter and LinkedIn for B2B (business to business). To get a better idea, ask your current clients what social media they participate in.

If you have a WordPress website, install a "Social Share" plug-in on your website for your blog posts or products (in the case of e-commerce websites). Using these buttons not only makes it easier for readers to share your content, but it will also be easier and quicker for you to share your own content on your social media accounts. These plug-ins often have the added benefit of letting you choose the thumbnail that will accompany the post on your Facebook page.

Sharing other people's content on your social media platforms is also a great way to provide value to your followers and get noticed by other people, businesses or organizations who may be more than happy to return the favor.

Another way to get backlinks is by joining in a discussion on public forums or commenting on other people's blogs and linking to your own website from the comment area. When used appropriately, readers of a blog will be interested to know if another site has additional information, or if there is a product or service that may be able to help them. These comments should be relevant to the conversation and add value. However, you must be careful not to post your URL just any old place, or you could get marked as a spammer. Once your domain has been marked as a spammer due to suspicious or unethical practices, it can be difficult to mend your tarnished reputation.

Beware of cheap backlinking services and "link farms." If a company promises hundreds of backlinks for only a few dollars, don't buy in to this! They will use sore thumb techniques such as spamming and possibly even hacking into other people's websites to get hundreds of links to your website.

If you have your own blog, you know that this is one of the primary targets of unscrupulous SEO companies. Here's how one of the tricks works: Their robots troll the Internet for blogs with public comment areas. They post a generic comment like "This blog is amazing!" and insert a link to their client's website. The owner of the blog, who doesn't know any better, will publish the comment thinking it is a real compliment from a fan. Then the client has a backlink from the blogger's website to theirs. The SEO firm does this hundreds (or thousands) of times over, using robots or overseas labor until they get the number of backlinks they promised.

As a blogger, delete these kind of comments and mark them as spam!

As a business owner, the most important thing is that you do not purchase one of these backlink/SEO packages no matter how desperate you might be! You might get a temporary spike in your rankings, but engaging in sketchy paid backlinking is almost certain to get you banned from Google.

CHAPTER 12

CONCLUSION

N ow you know the purpose of search engines and how they help people find information, products and services they are looking for.

You can find your way around a Search Engine Results Page. You understand why SEO and inbound marketing are taking the place of many outbound marketing strategies. You know the things you do on and off your website can help or hurt your SEO, depending on whether they are green thumb or sore thumb techniques. Let's review the important green thumb SEO concepts we've learned.

1. Create lots of high quality content using content marketing strategies to help drive visitors and keep them engaged for as long as possible.

2. Offer a wide variety of content while ensuring the content is relevant to your audience through keyword research.

3. Make it easy for people to find what they are looking for by providing a logical architecture and intuitive organization.

4. Maximize engagement and delight visitors with good design and visual content.

5. Foster easy access and use for the most number of visitors possible, keeping in mind site speed and usability on mobile devices.

6. Stick around in the same place long enough to allow things to develop and to leverage your longevity to gain authority.

7. Get as much buzz as possible from as many high profile places as you can by generating backlinks and social media interest.

Now that you have learned the basic concepts of Search Engine Optimization, you can get started today by simply writing down a list of 10 ideas you have for blog posts or content for your website. These ideas are the seeds you will sow and care for that will eventually bear you fruit.

Just like with gardening, if you have a little bit of knowledge, patience, the right tools and the motivation to work at it, you have what it takes to improve your search engine rankings. When done properly, you will see an enormous return on your investment.

If things seem confusing or unclear at times, just remember the garden. If it's good for the garden, it's probably good for your website!

Bibliography

Chapter 1

Sutter, John D. (2011). "How Many Pages Are on the Internet?"
www.cnn.com

Woollaston, Victoria (2013). "Revealed, What Happens in Just ONE Minute on the Internet"
www.dailymail.co.uk

Multiple sources (2015). "Total Number of Websites"
www.internetlivestats.com

Chapter 3

Lipsman, Andrew (2009). "comScore Releases June 2009 U.S. Search Engine Rankings"
www.comscore.com

Halligan, Brian and Shah, Dharmesh (2009). "Inbound Marketing: Get Found Using Google, Social Media, and Blogs"

Chapter 8

Robertson, Mark R. (2014). "2013 Online Video Marketing Survey and Business Video Trends Report"
www.reelseo.com

Chapter 9

Multiple authors (2012-2015). "Apple and Adobe Flash Controversy"
en.wikipedia.org

Chapter 10

Multiple sources (2015). "Total Number of Websites"
www.internetlivestats.com

About the Author

Candy Phelps is the digital marketing strategist and creative director of iCandy Graphics & Web Design. Candy has a bachelor of arts degree from the University of Montana and more than a decade of professional experience in graphic design, website development and marketing. Her search engine optimization experience was culled over years of developing websites, writing content and consulting for her business clients.

Candy is passionate about giving back to the community and helping other entrepreneurs succeed in following their dreams. She is also the founder of The Artery, an online art marketplace, as well as a co-founder of Sprout Landscape & Garden.

Candy hails from Montana originally and resides in Madison, Wisconsin with her husband, Tim, and their chickens, Maude, Ethel and Shirley. Candy enjoys art, bicycling, miniature gardening, playing the ukulele and being outdoors.

Connect

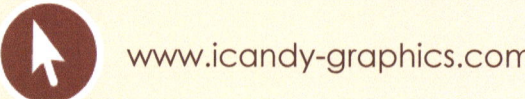 www.icandy-graphics.com

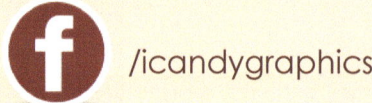 /icandygraphics

 @iCandyGraphics1

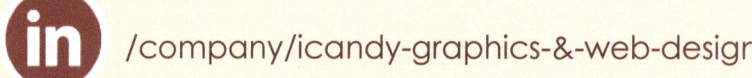 /company/icandy-graphics-&-web-design

 /icandygraphics

Free Resources!

Get additional resources, worksheets, helpful links and more to help you on you grow your SEO!

www.growyourseo.net

Password: seo-resources

Join the Conversation

#growyourseo #seogarden

www.ingramcontent.com/pod-product-compliance
Lightning Source LLC
Chambersburg PA
CBHW040829180526
45159CB00001B/120

* 9 7 8 1 5 1 1 8 5 7 1 9 2 *